Dance Dreams COLORING BOOK

VOLUME 3 - A BOYS BALLET ALPHABET

A Note from the Artist...

Thank you for purchasing Dance Dreams - Volume 3! As a dance teacher, I wanted to provide my male students with a ballet terminology learning tool designed especially for them, that would be engaging and inspiring. This book has been a valuable addition to my teaching syllabus for every level of study, and I'm happy to share it with you.

Each letter coloring page has a facing page, listing definitions, pronunciations and historical trivia. Some also have an inspiring note or thoughtful exercise geared toward younger dancers.

For the teacher, this book can work as a supplement to an existing syllabus, or become the basis for weekly classwork and discussion. The terms for many letters include beginner to advanced technical work, so you can choose which are appropriate for each class to focus on.

For the student, you can test yourself on spelling and definitions of the steps you know now, and ones that you will learn in the future. If there is a term you don't know, you can use the wealth of resource material available on the internet to see what you have to look forward to in your dance training. Some of the steps listed are for advanced level work, and require several years of study to attempt safely.

I hope this book inspires you in your ballet training!
Check in for free downloads, coloring lessons, and more at:
www.DanceDreamsInColor.com
Instagram: @Dance_Dreams_In_Color
Facebook: Dance Dreams Coloring Book

Come check out my YouTube reference portal
"Dance Dreams Coloring Book"
where I have personally collected playlists to go with each page of the coloring book.

I look forward to sharing other Dance Dreams with you!

Happy coloring! - Miss Kristine

$\mathscr{A}$ for...

Adagio	(a-DAHJ-e-o) At ease. In slow tempo.
en l'Air	(ahn-LEHR) In the air.
Allégro	(a-lay-GROH) Brisk or lively.
Allongé	(a-lawn-ZHAY) Extended, outstretched, elongated.
Arabesque	(ar-uh-BESK) Literally, "in Arabic fashion" - inspired by Moorish ornament. 
Assemblé	(a-sahm-BLAY) Assembled or joined together.
Attitude	(a-tee-TEWD) This pose was derived by Carlo Blasis from a statue of Mercury.
en Avant	(ahn-a-VAHNT) Forward direction

Artist's Note: You may wish to photocopy or scan the designs for yourself before you color, so you can return to them again and again! Place a clean sheet behind the page as you color and make sure you are working on a hard surface.
I recommend colored pencils or crayons on this paper.
I placed the terms and definitions in separate columns, so it would be easy for you to cover half with a piece of paper and test yourself on remembering them!
Have fun coloring and learning! - *Miss Kristine*

Arabesque

ALLONGÉ

en l'air

en AVANT

allégro

ASSEMBLÉ

ATTITUDE

ADAGIO

B for...

Balancé	(ba-lahn-SAY) Balanced.
Ballerina	(ba-lay-REE-nah) Originally a principal female dancer in a company.
Ballonné	(ba-law-NAY) Bouncing.
Ballotté	(ba-law-TAY) Tossed.

Mikhail Baryshnikov   (Born 1948, Latvia) Famous Russian-American dancer, choreographer, Artistic Director and actor. Cited as one of the greatest dancers in history, and more.

Barre	(bar) "An accessory, not a necessity!" Every ballet class begins with Barre.
Battement	(baht-MAHN) Beat. As in grand or petit.
Battu	(bah-TEW) A beat, usually added to step.
pas de Bourrée	(pah duh boo-RAY) Beating steps.

The English word "Ballet" is borrowed from the French, which came from the Italian "Balletto" (little ballet) derived from the Italian word "Ballaré" (to dance)!

GRAND
BATTEMENT

balancé
BATTU
BALLONÉ
ballotté
pas de bourrée

BARRE

EN BAS

C for...

Cabriole	(ka-bree-AWL) Caper, playful skip.
Cambré	(kahm-BRAY) Arched.
Changement de pieds	(shahn-zh-mahn duh pyey) Change of the feet.
Chaînés	(sheh-NAY) Chains, linked.
Chassé	(sha-SAY) To chase.
pas de Chat	(pah duh shah) Step of the cat.
en Cloche	(ahn clawsh) Like a bell.
Coupé	(koo-PAY) Cut or cutting.
Croisé	(cwah-zay) Crossed.
en Croix	(ahn cwah) In a cross.

Croisé

coupé

Châînés

CAMBRÉ

PAS DE

CHAT

changement

de pieds

CABRIOLE

en

CROÎX

chassé

# D for...

Premier Danseur	(dahn-SUHR) Leading male dancer of a company.
en Dedans	(ahn duh-DAHN) In the inward direction.
Dégagé	day-guh-zhay) Disengage.
en Dehors	(ahn day-oar) In the outward direction.
Demi-plié	(demee plee-yay) Half bend.
Derrière	(deh-ree-ehr) Back or behind.
Détourné	(day-toor-nay) Turned aside.
Devant	(day-vahn) In front.
Developpé	(Fr. dayv-law-pay) Developing movement.

Serge Diaghilev (1878-1929) Russian art critic, patron, ballet impresario and founder of the Ballet Russes, from which many famous dancers and choreographers would arise. He organized and financed many ballets, commissioning composers, costume designers and artists, to create some of the most influential ballets in history.

PREMIER
Danseur
développé
détourné
demi-plié
en
DEDANS
en
DEHORS
derrière devant
BATTEMENT
DÉGAGÉ

E for...

Ecarté   (ay-kar-TAY) Separated, thrown apart.

Echappé   (ay-shah-PAY) Escaping movement.

Effacé   (ay-fah-SAY) Shaded. Opposite of croisé.

Élancer   (ey-lahn-SAY) To dart. One of seven fundamental movements of the body codified in 1661 in France. See "K" for King Louis XIV to learn more!

Elevé   (el-eh-vay) To bring up. (Like an elevator!)

Emboîté   (ahm-bwah-TAY) Boxed, fit together.

Entrechat (ahn-truh-SHAH) Interweaving, braided.

Entrelacé (ahn-truh-luh-SAY) Interlaced.

Épaulment (ay-pohl-mahn) Shouldering.

Échappe
chappé
ÉCARTÉ
ÉLEVÉ
ÉPAULMENT
élancer
effacé
effacé
entrechat
entrelacé
Emboîté
enveloppé

F for...

en Face	(ahn fahss) Facing the audience.
Faille	(fi-yee) Giving way.
Fermé	(fair-may) Closed as in Sissone Fermé
First Position	Heels together, toes opened rotating the legs from the hips.
Flic-flac	(flick-flack) "Crack of a whip."
Fondu	(fawn-dew) Sinking down, melting.
Fouetté	(fweh-tay) Whipped.
Frappé	(frah-pay) Struck.

Mikhail Fokine (1880-1942) A groundbreaking Russian dancer and choreographer of the Imperial Ballet School, Ballet Russe and what was to become the American Ballet Theater. His pieces are still performed internationally. He choreographed works for the greatest dancers of his time, including *Pavlova* in the *The Dying Swan*, and *Nijinsky* in *Chopiniana* and *Les Sylphides*. He collaborated with many famous composers including *Rimsky-Korsakov, Stravinsky, Debussy* and *Offenbach*, to create new and exciting works.

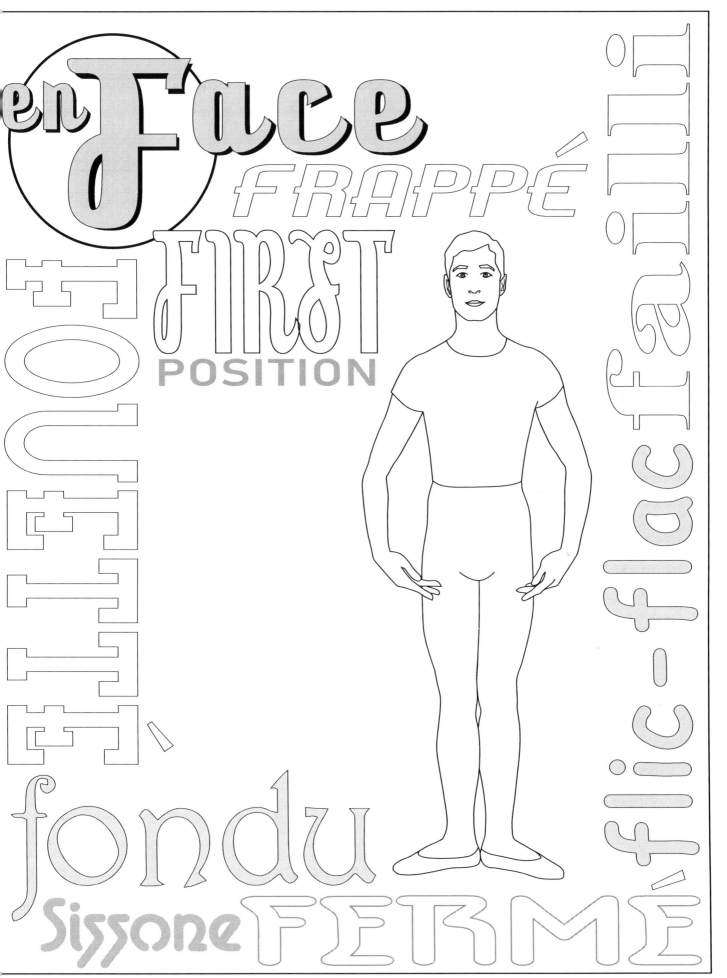

en **Face**

FRAPPÉ

First POSITION

fondu

Sissone FERMÉ

fliç-flac faillí

FOUETTÉ

ÉTTENDU

2020 Kristine Izak - Ballet Coloring Alphabet (Artist of Dance Dreams Coloring Book)

 for...

Galop	Named after the fastest running gait of a horse. Not a chasse!
Giselle	Famous Romantic Ballet first performed in1841 at the Paris Opera with Italian ballerina *Carlotta Grisi* as Giselle, a young peasant girl who falls in love and dies of heartbreak. *Lucien Petipa* danced the part of her lover, Albrecht. *Marius Petipa* staged a revival in the late 1890's that has been passed down to today.
Glissade	(glee-sod) Glide.
Grand Allegro	(grahnd) Big, large.
Grand Pas de Deux	(grahnd pah duh doo) Step of two. The most classic type, partners a male and female dancer and includes five sections that together tell a brief love story.

GRAND ALLEGRO

GRAND PAS DE DEUX

GALOP

Giselle

GLISSADE

# H for...

Harlequin (har-lah-kwin)

Les Millions d'Arelequin, also known as *Harlequinade*, is a ballet comique originally choreographed by *Marius Petipa* and presented in St. Petersburg by the Imperial Ballet in 1900. Two versions exist today, one performed primarily in Russia, and the other choreographed by *George Balanchine*, originally staged for the New York City Ballet.

The Italian *Commedia dell'arte* inspired the ballet. Harlequin, a comedic joker character, falls in love with Columbine, but her father does not approve and goes to great lengths to separate the two.

You can recognize Harlequin by his diamond patterned jacket, a black mask, and hat with bells or pom poms on it. Similar characters you might know are the Jack-in the-Box, and a Court Jester.

There is often a Harlequin and Columbine doll in the Nutcracker ballet as part of Herr Droselmeyer's entertainment for the party scene.

The dancing style of this character is very athletic, and often acrobatic too. If you like to tell jokes and pull pranks on people, you are an Harlequin at heart!

HARLEQUIN

I for... Inspiration!

Only if you love doing something can you be truly great at it. Dancing requires not just skill, but heart! You know those days when your "heart's just not in it." We all have those days! Think then about the days when you felt like you were flying, strong and fearless. All of these famous dancers had both kinds of days - but they didn't give up doing what they were passionate about.

Look to the library or internet for inspiration! Watch a video or read about one of these or other great dancers, then write a few lines about them that inspired you.

Mikhail Fokine
Serge Lifar
Rudolf Nureyev
Vaslav Nijinsky
Asaf Messerer
Mikhail Barishnikov
Anthony Dowell
Alexander Godunov
Erik Bruhn
Michel Descombey
Roberto Bolle
Benjamin Millepied
George de la Pena
Peter Martins
Arthur Mitchell
Carlos Acosta
Gerald Arpino
Michael Smuin
Daniel Sarabia
Steven McRae
Tetsuya Kumakawa
Sergei Polunin
Ivan Vasiliev

and many more!

The Dancer that inspired me was:

_____

These are things I learned about him:_____

_____

_____

_____

_____

_____

_____

_____

_____

_____

_____

2020 Kristine Izak - Ballet Coloring Alphabet (Artist of Dance Dreams Coloring Book)

 **for...**

Grand Jeté   (grahnd juh-tay) Big throw.

Petit Jeté   (puh-tee juh-tay) Small throw.

rond de Jambe   (rawn duh zhawm) Circle of the leg.

What is the difference between
a Grand Jeté and a Saut de Chat?

A Grand Jeté begins with a large battement
- or straight leg kick.

A Saut de Chat begins with a developpé.

In both jumps, the ultimate goal is a
beautiful split in the air!

GRAND JETÉ

petit JETÉ
rond de jambe

K for...

The Académie Royal de L'Danse was formed in Paris in 1661 by *King Louis XIV*. Courtiers learned to dance there and prepared large ballets as entertainment for the court. Can you guess who was the star of the show? The Sun King himself, of course! He proclaimed himself the center of the universe - and costumed as the sun, the ballets revolved around him.

King Louis was very proud of his shapely calves, and the open position we call turn-out was first performed by him to show off this feature. Together with his red high heeled shoes he stole the spotlight!

The jump, Royale, was named for the royal King. There is a legend that the King could not do an entrechat quatre jump very well, but he could manage the easier Royale. No one in the palace was allowed to perform the Royale except the King so no one would ever do it better than him! (It may be a true story, because it sounds like something the Sun King would do, doesn't it?)

Pierre Beauchamp (1631-1705), Director at the Académie Royal during King Louis' reign, is credited with being the first to codify the five positions of the feet in classical ballet. Dancers all over the world still use the five ballet positions today.
(See V for "Vaganova")

Sometimes, 6th position is described as "parallel first".
If you could design a 7th position what would it look like?

King Louis XIV
of France

The Sun King

le Roi Soleil

 for...

Temps Levé   (tahn luh-vey) Raised time. Hop on one foot.

Libretto   (lih-breh-toe) The text or story of the ballet or opera.

Temps Lié   (tahn lee-aye) Step to connect.

Line   Term that describes the outline of the dancer's body while performing steps or poses.

Fun fact:
Trapeze artist *Jules Leotard* made the "maillot" famous. It was designed for men, particularly those in the circus and acrobats. It wasn't until after his death that it was called a "leotard".

TEMPS LEVÉ

LIBRETTO

TEMPS LIÉ

TEMPS LIÉ

LINE

 for...

Manege   (ma-NEHJ) In a circle, as in Pique Manege

pas Marché   (pah mar-SHEY) A marching step.

Mazurka   (ma-ZUR-kuh) Polish folk dance featured in many classical ballets.

Arthur Mitchell (1934-201) American ballet dancer, choreographer and founder of *Dance Theater of Harlem*, the first African-American classical ballet company.

Ludwig Minkus (1826-1917) Famous composer for the St.Petersburg Imperial Theatre in Russia. His most celebrated compositions being the ballets *La Sylphide, Don Quixote, La Bayadere* and *Paquita*.

Note: Folk dances are represented in classical ballet in a stylized way adapted for the stage. They help set the scene and tell the story or "Libretto" of the ballet, as in Act II of *Swan Lake*. Often the dancers wear boots or high heeled shoes. Here are some other common Character Dance styles in ballet:
Polonaise (Poland)
Czardas (Hungary)
Tarantella (Italy)
Flamenco (Spain)
Kozachok, Hopak (Ukraine)
Gopak (Russia)

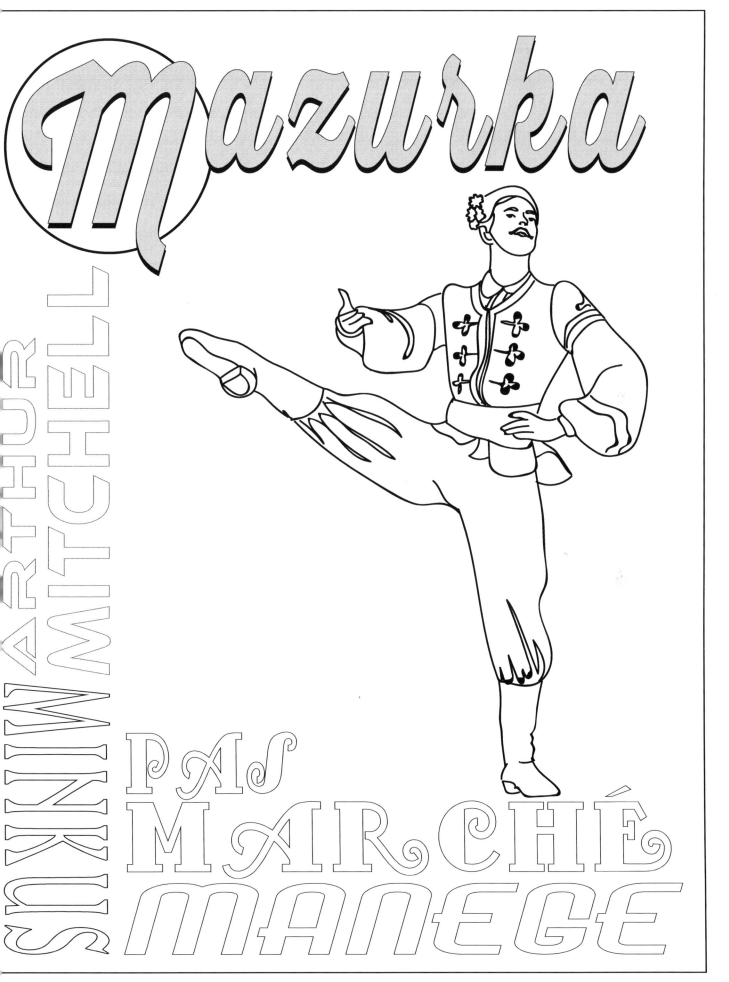

Mazurka

ARTHUR MITCHELL

MINKUS

PAS MARCHÉ MANEGE

N for...

Vaslav Nijinsky (1889-1950) Cited as the greatest dancer of the early 20th century, his technical virtuosity, together with his skill for creating characters with depth and intensity, made him a star performer and famous the world over. With the Ballet Russes he was able to experiment with choreography and music and created new directions for male dancers and modern ballet. Check out a photo of Nijinsky from his famous ballet, *The Afternoon of a Faun* (1912). He was a trailblazer!

Rudolf Nureyev (1938-1993) Called "Lord of the Dance" by many, he was considered the greatest dancer of his generation. He helped realize the role of male danseurs in their own right, not simply as a support for the prima ballerinas. He is also famous for his choreography and directorship of the Paris Opera Ballet. His last celebrated accomplishment was a new production of *La Bayadere* which in 1992, earned him France's highest cultural award.

The Nutcracker Ballet is based on E.T.A. Hoffman's fairy tale, *The Nutcracker and the Mouse King*. It tells the story of a little girl named Clara, who goes to the Land of Sweets on Christmas Eve. *Marius Petipa* and *Lev Ivanov* choreographed the first performance, in St. Petersburg, Russia in 1892. It is now one of the most popular ballets in the world, choreographed and staged in a variety of ways. The score, Op.71, by *Pyotr Illyich Tchaikovsky*, has become one of the composers most famous.

THE NUTCRACKER BALLET

VASLAV JINSKY

RUDOLF NUREYEV

O for...

Ouvert	(oo-VAIR) Open, as in Sissone Ouvert.
Ovation	A sustained and enthusiastic show of appreciation from an audience, especially by means of applause.
Overture	An orchestral piece at the beginning of a ballet, opera, suite, play, oratorio, or other extended composition.

O is for Opposites!
Can you draw a line between the words and
definitions in these pairs of opposites in ballet terminology?

Ouvert
Fermé
  en L'air
  par Terre
Grand(e)
Petit(e)
  en Haut
  en Bas
Devant
Derrière
  en Avant
  en Arrière
Dessous
Dessus

Back
In the low position.
In the forward direction.
Open
Small
Under
In the air.
In the high position.
Front
In the backward direction.
Over
Large
On the ground.
Closed

SISSONE
OUVERT

overture

ovation

P for...

Pas	(pah) Step...
de Basque	of the Basque (region between Spain and France).
de cheval	of the horse.
Passé	(pay-SAY) To pass
Anna Pavlova	(1881-1931) Famous Russian prima ballerina most recognized for her role as The Dying Swan. First ballerina to tour around the world.
Penché	(pawn-SHAY) Leaning.
Petit or Petite	(puh-tee, puh-teet) Small.
Pirhouette	(peer-o-wet) Spin.
Piqué	(pee-kay) Pricked.
Plié	(plee-ay) To bend.
Port de Bras	(poor-t duh braw) Carry the arms.
Portée	(poor-tay) Carry.
Premier Danseur	(pray-meeyear dahn-sur) Leading male dancer in a company. Like a Prima Ballerina for ladies.
Promenade	(prom-en-odd) A walk.

Plié

Anna Pavlova

Port de Bras

PIQUÉ

PORTÉE

POLKA

Passé

PETIT

ALLEGRO

Pirhouette

DE BASQUE

DE CHEVAL

PAS

PROMENADE

penché

Q for...

Entrechat Quatre   (ahn-truh-shah ka-tra) Interweave beat the legs four times.

Pas de Quatre   (pah duh ka-tra) Dance or step for four.

Quatrième Derrière (ka-tree-em dare-ee-yair) Fourth in back. Referring to a position of the feet.

Don Quixote   (don key-hoe-tay)
Very famous comical ballet originally choreographed by *Marius Petipa* in 1869, based on the novel by Miguel Cervantes. Nicknamed "Don Q in the ballet scene, the ballet has very athletic roles for both men and women. Performed around the world and appreciated for it's many challenging solo variations and great music by *Ludwig Minkus*.

*See also C for Croisé

Quatrieme
DERRIÈRE

Don Quixote

entrechat quatre

PAS DE QUATRE

R for...

Raccourci	(ra-coor-see) Shortened.
Relevé	(re-luh-vay) Raised.
Renversé	(rahn-ver-say) Reversed.
Retiré	(reh-tee-ray) Withdrawn. A position.
Rivoltade	(reh-vol-tawd) To turn over.
Retombé	(reh-tawm-bay) Falling back.
Rond de jambe	(rawn duh zhawm) Circle of the leg.
Royale	(roh-YAL) A jump where the dancer beat the legs in the air once before changing position of the feet when landing. (See "K" for King Louis)

RETIRÉ

Relevé

RIVOLTADE

Renversé

retombé

RONDE

ROYALE

de jambe

Raccourci

2020 Kristine Izak - Ballet Coloring Alphabet (Artist of Dance Dreams Coloring Book)

S for...

Saut de chat de Basque	(soh duh shah) Cat's jump. (soh duh bahsk) Basque jump.
Sauté	(so-tay) Jumped.
à la Seconde	(ah la suh-GAWND) To the side or second position.
Sissone	(see-sawn) Named after Alfred Sissone, the inventor of this step!
Solo	A dance for one person.
Soubresaut	(su-bruh-so) Quick spring.
Soutenu	(soo-teh-new) Sustained.
Spotting	A word to describe the action of a dancer's head when turning.
Sus-sous	(su-sue) Over-under.

La Sylphide   First ever Romantic Ballet (Italy, 1831). Choreographed by *Filippo Taglioni* for his daughter Marie. *Joseph Mazilier* created and performed the lead role of James in 1831. He was most noted for his ballets *Paquita* and *Le Corsaire*. The second version, choreographed by *Auguste Bournonville* (Denmark, 1836) is one of the oldest surviving ballets.

Sus-sous
SOLO
SAUTÉ
à la
Seconde
à la
spotting
Soutenu
SAUT de Chat
DE BASQUE
SOUBRESAUT
La Sylphide
SISSONE

T for...

Marie Taglioni	Romantic ballerina - first to go en pointe and to wear a tutu (La Sylphide
Tarantella	A folk dance of Italy characterized by light, quick steps.

Technique The principles of body movement, with emphasis on method and execution. These include alignment, turn-out, clean footwork, toe pointing, grace, dynamic quality of movement, correct body positions and posture, lines and angles, and much more!
(See also "V" for Ballet Methods.)

Tendu	(tahn-doo) Stretched or held tautly.
Temps Lié	(tahn lee-aye) Step to connect.
Tombé	(tawm-bay) To fall.
Tour	(tour) A turn.
en Tournant	(on tour-non) In a turning way.
Turn-out	Outward rotation of the legs from the hip joint.

TENDU

TEMPS LIÉ

TOUR

TECHNIQUE

en Tournant

TAGLIONI

STRETCH

tarantella en l'air

TOMBÉ

TURN OUT

Choose a friend or classmates you admire.
Write four reasons why...

_____

_____

_____

_____

What are four things a friend might admire about you?
What do you admire about yourself?
(Don't be shy - remember there is only one You in the entire Universe!)

_____

_____

_____

_____

What would you want your teacher to say to you,
to encourage you in your dancing?

_____

_____

_____

(Repeat this to yourself when you need a lift!)

UNIQUE

"There is a vitality, a life force, a quickening that is translated THROUGH YOU INTO ACTION and because there is only ONE of YOU in ALL TIME, this expression is UNIQUE, and if you block it, it will never exist through any other medium, and be LOST. The world will not have it. It is not your business to determine how good it is, not how it compares with other expression. It is your business to keep it yours clearly and directly, to KEEP THE CHANNEL OPEN."

— Martha Graham

How it all started...from feet to fundamentals!

Pierre Beauchamp (1631-1705) is credited with being the first to arrange according to a system, the five positions of the feet in classical ballet. His method of writing down and drawing movement steps and poses was printed in 1700. It was used to record dances for the stage and for social dancing, like parties and balls. He was director of the Académie Royale de Danse and gave lessons to *King Louis XIV* for over twenty-two years. He also choreographed and composed music for ballets starring the King and his court at Versailles. (See K for "King Louis XIV")

Ballet's major training systems (listed to the right) all use Beauchamps's original five positions of the feet. However, the schools have different names for the positions of the arms, epaulment, some steps, arabesques, and more.
It can get confusing!
(See H for "en Haut")

Here are The Seven Fundamentals of Movement
first described by Beauchamps:

1. Plier   - to bend
2. Étendre   - to stretch toe,ankle and knee into a straight leg
3. Glisser   - to glide
4. Relever   - to rise, on the balls of your feet or en pointe
5. Sauter   - to jump, strongly, and land softly!
6. Tourner   - to turn around
7. Élancer   - to dart, jump, along or just above the floor

You probably know a step from each of these fundamentals!

Vaganova
RUSSIAN

l'École Française
FRENCH

Cecchetti
Italian

Bournonville
DANISH

R.A.D.
BRITISH

BALANCHINE
AMERICAN

for...

Waltz - From the German word "Walzen" which describes the rolling nature of the dance.

Every classical ballet has a waltz in it, and many have two or three! You can recognize them by the tempo of the music - 3 beats per measure - and usually there are many dancers on stage, and often couples.

Here are a few famous ballet waltzes that you can watch online. You might also play the music, and try dancing a waltz of your own!

La Bayadère - Minkus

Cinderella - Prokofiev

Coppélia - Delibes

Don Quixote - Minkus

Giselle - Adam

The Nutcracker Ballet - Tchaikovsky

Raymonda - Glazunov

The Sleeping Beauty Ballet - Tchaikovsky

Swan Lake - Tchaikovsky

Waltz
Pas de Valse

3/4

Why do we say UP-stage and DOWN-stage when the floor of the stage is flat?

Ballet was first performed on stages designed for the opera - and for singers and actors. The stages could be "raked" or tilted with big cranks so that the voices in the back of the stage could be heard over the heads of the performers in front. Dancers at one time needed to practice in studios that were "raked" too, so that they could learn to distribute their body weight to be able to balance,turn and jump without falling. Like dancing on a hill!
Can you imagine that?
The back of the stage was REALLY up
and the front REALLY down!

Some people or things you
might see when you are
on stage:

Spotlights
Footlights
Trees
Sight lines
Marley Floor
Rosin
Syc or Backdrop
Fly Space
Orchestra Pit
Stage Manager
Wardrobe Assistant

Getting ready to perform?
The difference between a
good dancer, and
a great dancer,
is attention to...
Performance Quality
Projection
Focus
Spatial Awareness
Movement Memory
Commitment
Concentration
& Confidence!

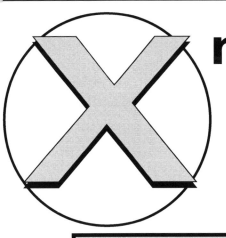

marks the spot:
CENTER STAGE

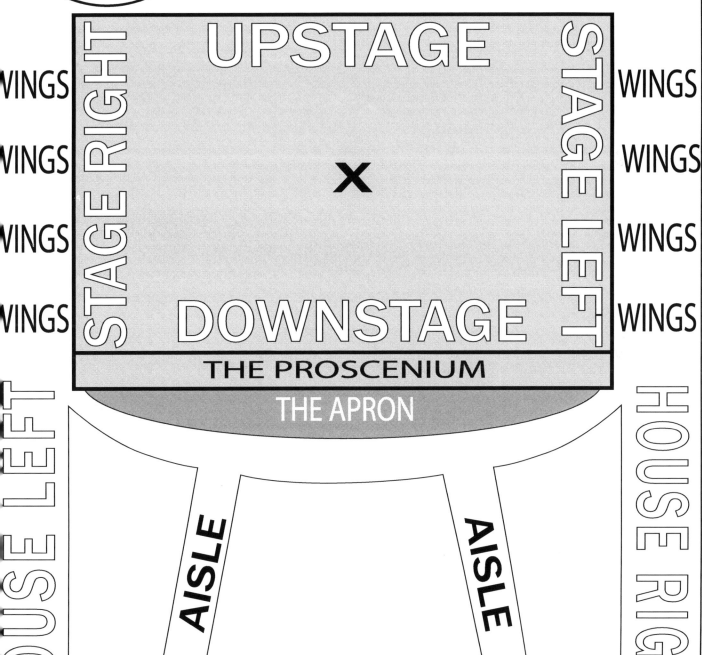

UPSTAGE

X

DOWNSTAGE

THE PROSCENIUM

THE APRON

STAGE RIGHT

STAGE LEFT

WINGS

WINGS

WINGS

WINGS

WINGS

WINGS

WINGS

WINGS

HOUSE LEFT

HOUSE RIGHT

AISLE

AISLE

Dancers from the ballet "Les Sylphides" - notice the fitted vest on the male dancer here?

EVOLUTION OF MALE DANCEWEAR FOR REHEARSAL AND PERFORMANCE...

1600's - King Louis XIV time...Men wore heels (yes, high heels!) and stiff bell shaped skirts, knee breeches, wigs, and swords belted at the waist.

1790 - The invention of tights, although mostly worn by women.

1820 - Carlo Blasis designed male dancewear so as not to conceal the outline of the body: a tight fitting jacket and trousers of white cloth, and a wide black leather belt tightly buckled around the waist.

1826 - The trousers replaced by shorter knee breeches and silk socks. Auguste Bournonville invents the male slipper - black with a white V shaped vamp in front.

1844 - Men have replaced the jacket with short vests at the Paris Opera Ballet allowing for greater range of motion.

1859 - Acrobat Jules Leotard popularizes the one-piece maillot - later called the "Leotard"

1911 - Nijinksy danced Giselle in St. Petersburg. His costume caused a scandal because he danced for the first time on stage in tights without the then-common breeches. Dance belts have been an essential part of the male dancers attire since possibly back to Nijinksy's time. For certain, since 1930, the design has developed with the invention of more supportive and stretchable fabrics.

'Why' do you Love Ballet?
How do you feel when you dance?
What is your favorite part of class?
What are you most proud
                    of in your dancing?

I love Ballet because... _____

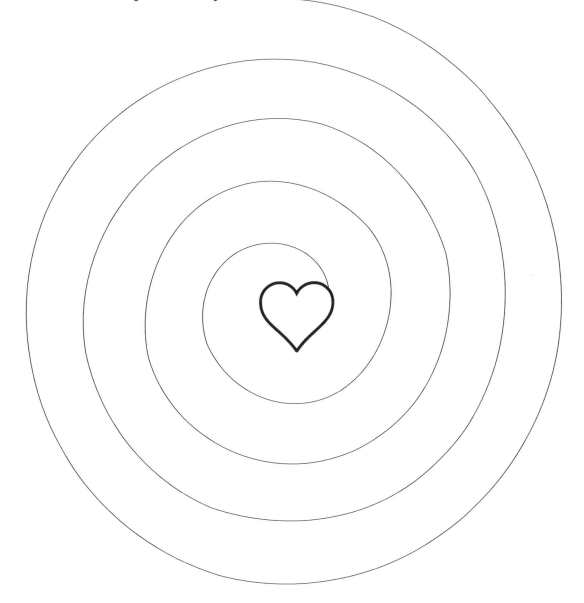

Start from the outside of the circle and write your answers towards the center heart.
Then you get to the center heart, you can start your way out again by writing on the bottom of the line.

Coda	The concluding section of a dance, especially of a pas de deux or the finale of a ballet.
Curtain Call	The final bow. Occurs at the end of a performance. May include recognizing the choreogapher, director and conductor.
Encore	An additional performance given after the planned show has ended, usually in response to extended applause by the audience!
Finalé	The last part of a ballet, usually dramatic and exciting.
Révérence	The last exercise of a ballet class, usually includes a bow (for men) and curtsy (for ladies) and port de bras. Students pay respect and ackowledge their teacher and accompanist if there was one.

Breaking a leg?
The phrase may be traced back to Shakespeare's time, when to bow, you had to bend or 'break' your leg. Since a successful performance ended with a bow and applause, wishing an actor "Break a Leg!"is a wish for their good luck!

Some dancers are very superstitious and prefer you say "Merde" to them. ("Merde" translates as 'poop' in French!) If there was a full house, that meant lots of carriages and horses in front of the theater...and lots of poop! If someone says "Merde" to you - the response is "Oui!" which means 'yes.'

Do you have any superstitions or things you always do before a show that you believe bring you good luck?_____
_____
_____

Zee END!

Révérence

BOW

curtsy

Finalé

ENCORE

STANDING

OVATION

CODA

APPLAUSE!

CURTAIN CALL

Dear Dancers,

I hope you had fun coloring through the Ballet Alphabet with me!
I think those of us who dance belong to a special secret club. We
know a joy that comes from training our bodies to move in marvelous
ways, that is hard to put into words. Never take for granted the gift of
a dancing spirit you have been given, and remember,
you were born to dance!

If you would like to color more of my art, you can purchase
Volume 1 - In Your Element, in my Etsy shop, and on Amazon.

Volume 2 - A Ballet Alphabet is also available, and similar in content
to Vol.3, except the images are of girls and ladies.

Visit my website to link up to my Etsy shop, subscribe for free
downloads, updates on publications, coloring contests and more!
www.dancedreamsincolor.com

Follow me on Instagram
@dance_dreams_in_color

Join me on Facebook
Dance Dreams In Color
Dance Dreams Coloring Book

Check out playlists for every page
of the coloring book on YouTube -
Dance Dreams Coloring Book

You can also color along with
me on the YouTube channel!

Please keep dancing
and loving what you do!
Until the next Dance Dreams journey,

Miss Kristine

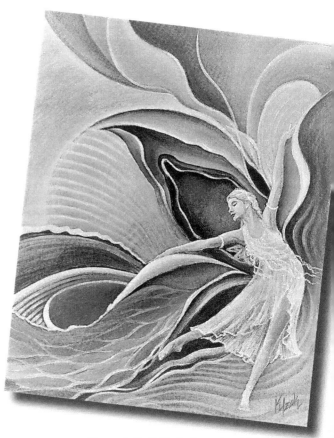

"Inspirita" Painting by Kristine Izak

Tear out this blank page and place it under the page your are coloring.
You can also use it for notes or drawings of your own!

Printed in Great Britain
by Amazon